100 Pearls and Gems

OLAREWAJU OLADIPO

First Printing, March 2019

FOREWORD

100 Pearls and Gems is the third book of a collection of literary work expressing the inner thoughts of the author, as it is shaped by the events of the day and encounters with both the living and non-living. It is my hope and desire that you, the reader, will find use in this book that far exceeds my imagination.

ACKNOWLEDGEMENT

This book is dedicated to all those who continue to support our work at 3SqMeals.

The most perfect of all humans is utterly imperfect in its most beautiful state. Human imperfection is a universal gift to mankind, one that drives our innate desire for an unattainable ideal. To comprehend the inherent beauty of your imperfection is to acknowledge your creation.

An unrecognized miracle and an unfulfilled miracle have one thing in common: they rarely warrant a need for gratitude from the person in need.

Treat every encounter as a predestined meeting, and you will never miss your opportunity to be somebody's angel. There is no better earthly conduit for timely miracles than through a fellow human.

To forget where you came from is to confuse where you are in your journey with your destination. Nothing molds a destiny like its beginning.

Do not let your preoccupation with leadership distract you from the needs and desires of the people you aspire to represent. The purest way to lead is to lead from the heart and aspire to connect with the hearts of all those who follow you.

The opposite of failure is not always success, for it is possible to achieve great success in one dimension of life and be a flop in another.

To see with the eyes of elders is to be endowed with a vision beyond what is visible to the physical eyes. The blindness of youth is not a curse but a reason to embrace the wisdom of those who came before you.

The most lethal form of change within occurs when unrecognized self-transformation happens to the detriment of self and all those around you.

To cast your burden is to disallow your fear to dictate your thought. To cast your burden is to denounce the evil that makes a hell out of your troubles. To cast your burden is to discover a future beyond your pain. To cast your burden is to decide not to fight your battle alone.

To bask in extreme ignorance is to be immersed in total darkness and be utterly convinced of seeing a life-size reflection of your own shadow.

You can never be too poor to give, for deep in your heart is the greatest gift of all: love. You can never be too rich to receive, for no one has enough of the greatest gift of all: love.

To surrender to be led by others is no license to be dependent on them. To volunteer to lead others is no liberty to be independent of them.

You are one second away from hope, one minute away from peace, one hour away from joy, one week away from contentment, one month away from resolution, one year away from purpose, one lifetime away from fulfillment, one generation away from legacy and not the opposites.

The secret to truly owning one hundred percent of anything worth owning is to share it in one hundred ways and let it bring forth its seeds.

The message of love is like melody to the ears that makes you want to hear the song played a thousand times. If only the world will choose to listen endlessly to the song filled with the message of love, no one will ever feel empty again.

The test of friendship is hardly in the material things you have to offer but simply in being human when a friend is at the lowest of spirit.

Experience is no substitute for knowledge; knowledge is no substitute for wisdom; wisdom is no substitute for grace; grace is no substitute for hope; hope is no substitute for faith; faith is no substitute for belief; belief is no substitute for love; love has no real substitute.

The perception of self as beautiful should not be a momentary thought but a perpetual feeling that admires one's evolution from year to year.

In every moment of joy is an opportunity to make the experience last as long as possible in your memory. In every moment of sadness is an opportunity to make the experience last as short as possible in your memory. Exercise your dominion over joy and sadness, and not vice versa.

To navigate the maze of life, acknowledge the incomprehensible, respect the extraordinary, believe the impossible, and define your own path.

The intrinsic value of failing in an endeavor lies beyond the personal experience of a disappointment and a lesson on how to better cope with failure, but in the opportunity it presents to ensure that there is no repeat of the same mistake.

A minute of silence is a must when you pause to see who is here and who was once here. Observe this every day, and you will never walk alone.

You can never rely solely on your thought of self, for who you think you are is not always who people think you are. Somewhere in between who you think you are and who others think you are is the real you.

To be absent in your presence is to pass through this world like a willful bystander; to be present in your absence is to pass through this world like an active explorer. The legacy of life—joy and peace—belong to those who see their world as a planet waiting to be discovered.

Your wisest words are the words
you intentionally reserve for your
ears. You do not always have to
say a word to make a world of
difference.

To live your tomorrow today is to allow greed to take the better part of you and to forfeit a promising but yet to-be-realized future for the pleasures of today. The true price of tomorrow is never defined until today is fully spent.

Purpose is a shifting target that is possible only after meeting set goals. You are unlikely to fulfill your purpose without setting a goal.

The journey of a thousand years is not designed for one person to run but for one person to begin. What you do with the baton of legacy is not to hold on to it indefinitely but to make sure you are not the last person to gain possession of it.

Passion without a vision is like paddling a canoe aimlessly down a river. Anyone can have a drive, but not everyone knows where they are going.

To fully appreciate the beauty of life, you always have to adjust your vision to capture the beauty of mankind in all the things, good or bad, that manifest in your world.

The most vicious of all thieves are those who make it their mission to steal other peoples' joy. You really deserve your joy; don't lose it.

To lead when you are lost is a disservice to those who see you as their leader; to submit to be led by a leader without a direction is a disservice to self. To lead is not a birthright to majority but a badge of honor worn only by those who see leadership as a service to mankind.

Many people long for life, but not everyone longs to live. How you live your life on Earth matters more than the count of your years on Earth.

You may never find a reason to forgive one another, but you will always hear the voice of reason through the act of forgiveness.

Whenever you have a reason to complain about others, use the moment to remember all those who truly deserve your compliment but never got it.

To rely solely on personal ability to achieve set goals is to limit the possibility of your being and put a cap on what is achievable. To make the gains of your effort infinite, never forget to explore the power of collaboration.

Begin the day with a spirit of gratitude. End the day with a spirit of expectancy. Through the day, be thankful for what is yet to manifest.

The body has a mind; the mind has a body. To lose your mind is to be absent but not absent; to lose your body is to be present but not present.

If failure is a communicable disease, many will opt for a vaccine to eliminate the malady. Failure is not for everyone, but no one is immune.

A hero never has a choice of the moment to act out their courage, but the call to engage the moment is motivated by an unwavering sense of duty, a commitment to service, a selfless devotion to the pursuit of justice, and a desire to stand up for the cause of a fellow human.

To critic more than you commend
is to consciously choose to only
see just one color out of the many
colors that make up the rainbow of
life.

Though we may travel the same path, our journeys are less defined by that which is common to us but that which is tailored to our destinies.

To recognize how little you know about how the next minute will turn out is to understand the limit of your being. To live in the moment is to not take life too seriously and to live life to the fullest.

There is plenty of time when your sole existence is to serve you. There is not enough time when you define your existence by serving others.

To talk more than you listen is to miss the tangible whispers of life. For those life pearls that are never spoken aloud, you have to listen.

Be careful not to confuse the limit you set for yourself with the limit set for you by others. No limit is as binding as the one you accept.

To live in abundance is to enjoy peace in the midst of chaos, to give thanks when there is a reason to complain, to find contentment in the battle to survive, to be able to give out of a little, to respect the sacrifice of those gone by, and to spare a moment to laugh through pain.

Many great achievements in life are simply the rewards for trying. Many great feats in life are simply the prizes for showing up. So simple.

What you see with the eyes is never all that is visible to the eyes, for it is only human to set eyes on the things that one desires to see.

Your control over the future is limited to the pursuit of your imagination. To pursue your imagined future, you have to embrace your reality.

Love is meaningless if the love of
thy neighbor is set a bar below the
love of you and yours. Love based
on preset terms is not
unconditional love.

Not to be defined by your achievements is to give it your all to achieve it, but be willing to give it up without feeling like you are lost.

To embrace greed for the sake of others is to forgo greed for the sake of self. Let the desire for more be for a reason other than your want.

To some legacy is an inheritance; to some legacy is unintentional; to some legacy is intentional. Not all lasting legacies are created equal.

Little things—a simple smile, an ordinary prayer, a friendly note, an unexpected call, a short visit, a positive gesture, a thankful message, a beautiful flower, a shared moment, an encouraging chat, a memorable trip, a listening ear, a timely tea, a simple nod. Little things.

You cannot conquer bigotry with bigotry. You cannot win a lost soul by sacrificing yours. Be one to shine a ray of light when darkness looms.

The constant fear of ignorance is
the sustainable path to wisdom.
What you believe you know has a
potential to become your biggest
liability.

Hatred is never justified no matter what your prevailing circumstance is. To hate a fellow human being is to double your emotional suffering.

Whatever your desire is in life, do not let it enslave you. Whatever your ambition is in life, do not let it imprison you. Whatever your purpose is in life, do not let it dehumanize you.

The measured is not always treasured until its impermanence is imminent. Treat every treasure with a mind that it may one day cease to exist.

The power to become significant is less to do with your talent but more to do with the benevolence of those whose paths intersect with yours.

It's possible to win a battle and still feel like a loser. It's possible to have it all and still feel empty. Fulfillment is a spice of life.

The person with unrecognized talents or gifts is very much like the person with unrealized talents or gifts; what separates the two are the people that see the talent in the talented and make it their life purpose to champion their cause. Without a champion, talent is only talent.

Love is simple; love is complex.
Love is palpable; love is fluid. Love
abound; love is close. Love is true;
love is real. Love thyself first.

The timing of a breakthrough is never in the hand of man, but it demands everyone in need of a breakthrough to seek it with all their might.

This day is yours to claim or squander, to embrace or flounder, to ignore or ponder, to reveal or launder, to fulfill or surrender, to hoard or render. This day is yours.

To rely only on instinct is to surrender sense. To rely only on sense is to forfeit instinct. A little instinct, a little sense saves the day.

Tomorrow is a blank canvas
waiting to fulfill our imagination.
Tomorrow is an empty glass cup
waiting to receive our thoughts.
Tomorrow is a closed door waiting
to reveal new possibilities.
Tomorrow is a night train waiting
to begin an adventure.
Tomorrow is for dreamers.

There is always a price—a price for doing, a price for not doing, and a price for undoing. Do something if the price for not doing is high.

Happiness is an earthly desire; peace is a heavenly gift. Those who make the pursuit of peace their earthly desire always discover happiness.

Do not let a morbid preoccupation with finding your purpose be a barrier to the joy of doing things that do not seem to matter in the moment.

If you wait to be led, you may never begin your journey. If you wait to be followed, you may never continue your journey. If you wait to be cheered, you may never end your journey. The journey of a lifetime begins with no prompt, continues with no company, and ends with no cheer.

Many discoveries are revelations of
what already exist but were
previously unappreciated. Your
true purpose is always within your
proximity.

Human endeavors are full of surprises, but no surprise beats that which we engender in ourselves.

A smile may fool the unsuspecting of the emotion within, but conversation will open the door of pretense and offer a glint of the pain within.

Do not let the fear of the unknown rob you of the pleasure of a better future. No one knows tomorrow, but everyone aspires to see another day.

Hope takes different forms in its earthly manifestation. False hope is when a man tells himself to rely on self as a source. Lost hope is when a man witnesses the disappearance of their earthly source. The closest one can come to hopelessness is to rely on another man as a source.

Be a river of blessing that flows through a multitude of people, watering its surroundings and enabling every seed in its ground to flourish.

The discovery of the world of self is incomplete without an exploration of the ocean of attitude. The journey of self-discovery never begins with self.

To seed into your life is to sacrifice a portion of you in return for a future desired but not guaranteed. To seize the future, sow the seed.

Vision is what you see when there
is no light; the house you build
when there is no land; the dream
you pursue when there is no hope;
the journey you begin when there
is no map; the cup you hold when
there is no water; the painting you
see when there is no canvas—it's a
vision.

If you are seeking the truth, remember the wonder of a mirror. There is no better way to find the truth than looking at a reflection of self.

Fearlessness is not the equivalent of bravery, failure is not the equivalent of hopelessness.

To lend an ear is to listen with the intention to immerse yourself into a world as experienced by the person seeking your undivided attention.

The similarity between knowledge and understanding is that both are constantly changing. The difference between knowledge and understanding is that knowledge at its best can only offer you new information while understanding will reveal how best to use the information at hand.

To lend a hand is to resolutely engage oneself in a selfless pursuit of good for the sake of the person in need of your unmerited assistance.

In your quest for survival do not squander your legacy; in your quest for legacy do not sacrifice your being. The opportunity to build a legacy is limited without first mastering the art of survival.

To be broken-hearted is not the same as being broken—one takes a part of you; the other takes the whole of you. Let the whole of you rule.

Influence is like a fire that spares no one. Some see its flame from afar, some nearby feel the heat, some up-close get singed, and the less fortunate suffers burns of varying depth. Every dose of influence has a potential to have an impact far greater than one could ever anticipate.

When your only option is what you once thought was impossible, you gain possession of the key that opens the door to an extraordinary future.

Just like you have no control over the passing of time, physical change is inevitable over time. Just like physical change occurs one second at a time until it becomes apparent to all, personal growth occurs one moment at a time until you become the person you aspire to be.

Finding the door is not as important as finding the right key to open it and definitely less important than having the right person open it.

Imagination pursued at the expense of true reality is the beginning of disaster. What separates your imagination from your reality is sanity.

Let sunrise be a reminder of how little you know; let sunset be a reminder of how much more there is to know. Acknowledge personal ignorance.

Timeliness of success is a rarity, as no one likes to wait when instant success is possible on preferential terms. Time is often a price to pay if you dare to succeed; the alternative is always available to those who are impatient, unwilling to put in the effort and stay the course.

You do the same thing everyday.
You do the same thing
everyday for the same reason.
You do the same thing everyday
for the same result.
Why?

Your dream is not big enough until
it has the power to enable others
to dream big. Hope comes alive
when the least amongst us are
made to see what is possible.
If you can breathe, it ain't over.

Hope is not lost when you cannot see. Hope is not lost when you cannot hear. Hope is not lost when you cannot feel. Hope is not lost when you cannot walk. Hope is not lost when you cannot talk. If you can breathe, it ain't over.

Do not consider yourself to have done enough good if all the good you have done is for the benefits of only the people you know or have met.

The desire to navigate the obstacle course of life despite what the season says defines living.

You can always fake happiness or make happiness. To the outside world, the authenticity of your happiness is secure; to you, the purity of life's greatest emotion is lost. Happiness is not about how you like the outside world to see you but how you like to see your inner world.

ABOUT THE AUTHOR

Olarewaju Oladipo is an author (fiction and non-fiction) whose writing career began while practicing as an orthopedic surgeon. Following the release of his earlier books "The White Coat" (2006) and "House Calls" (2007), he dedicated the next few years to crafting motivational quotes written using the Twitter handle @3SqMeals as Dr. O' and publishing multiple books under the '3SqMeals Tweets – Not Your Typical Meal' series.

His works of fiction include the "North Main Street" mystery series and the "Once A Doc" medical fiction series, with the release of Barber's Haven (2015), 'A Patient called Emma' (2015) and 'Ghost Bus (2016).

'The Sculpture Garden' series is based on actual sculptures and part of an ongoing effort to support the work of local artists in Nigeria, fund the establishment of sustainable sculpture gardens, and sponsor worldwide collaborations with art institutions.

Two Blind Men (2017) was the first of a collection of short stories of the 'Sculpture Garden' series. Tortoise of Many Colors (2017), The Tree of Wonder (2017), and Esther (2018) are other books in the series.

100 Prayers and Whispers (2018) is the first book in a series devoted to daily reflections of the author as shared using a dedicated Twitter handle - @3SqMeals.

All books are available in paperbacks and eBook formats on Amazon, Kobo, Smashwords, and on author's website (www.olarewajuoladipo.com).